KALEIDOSCOPES & CRYSTALS

POEMS BY PAT COUGHLIN-MAWSON

I gratefully acknowledge Debbie Mullen
and Judy Sumrell for their illustrations in this book.

For information, address correspondence to:

Pat Coughlin-Mawson
1400 Augusta Drive
Savannah, Texas 76227

ISBN 1453859314
ISBN-13 9781453859315

TABLE OF CONTENTS

THE GARDEN

Will you take this walk with me
  Into the garden, and you will see

Gentle colors, morning mist
  Can you slowly take the risk?

Let go of stories that keep you old
  Let go of feelings never told

Hear the rain, its gentle mist
  Hear the river and its twists

Touch the flowers, colored bright
  See the bird's majestic flight

Walk down the path of scary nights
  Fall to the ground, and see new sights

See the sky of deepest blue
  Feel the beauty inside of you

Come down this path and you will see
  A newer, freer way to be.

JJ 9-11-10

KALEIDOSCOPES AND CRYSTALS

Kaleidoscopes and crystals
　　Possibilities or dreams
Colors in the distance
　　Of beauty rarely seen

Childlike wonder mirrors
　　Spreading rainbows on my mind
Inviting me to distant paths
　　Of many other times

Take the time to ponder
　　Take the time to see
The beauty and the wonder
　　Dancing deeply inside me

And if I stay here long enough
　　I will begin to find
A kaleidoscope of colors
　　Right inside my mind

Can I take them with me
　　Can I take my mind
Beyond these earthly pleasures
　　Where there is no space or time?

Can I take the beauty
That I've worked so hard to see
　　Can I take my memories
Beyond the ocean seas?

For when my time has come at last
   To leave these earthly walls
I'll open up to freedom
   And gaze and stare with awe

At kaleidoscopes and crystals
   All throughout the lands
And fly amidst their colors
   And know the larger plan.

IF I COULD ONLY

If I could only find the pain
   Release the fear, let go of shame

If I could only trust my heart
   To look within the many parts

To ask myself—what's right for me
   To come together, to once feel free

To begin to love, instead of need
   So much from others

I could begin to touch the joy
   Of every other girl and boy

I could begin to dance with glee
   And trust the many parts of me

To look within and end the blame
   Let go of anger, guilt and pain

To Live life free
   And just be me

And simply give.

THIS DAY

We only have
  This brand new day
Fresh air to breathe
  Kind words to say

Colors bright
  And sounds so new
And so I give
  My love to you

Love so gentle
  And so strong
To blanket you
  As you go on

We only have
  This smile to give
This time right now
  This love to live

We only have *this* day!

MINUTES

Minutes slowly passing by
  Without permission time just flies

We gain wisdom from this place
  Of passing moments – hidden grace

So every minute – another try
  As minutes slowly click right by

Our story gives us inner strength
  To make changes with our paints

Our canvas will become the gift
  We leave behind – and slowly lift
    Our souls to comfort.

MORNING PRAYER

As the beauty of this day begins
   I no longer dream what might have been
I welcome morning with her light
   Breathe in her air with all my might

I move with hopeful brand new steps
   Not looking back with regrets
For each old story had its place
   I learn to walk a future pace

Where all the choices now are mine
   I co-create with all the minds
      Until we all are One

And any time I need to go
   Back to the place before I know
I close my eyes and go inside
   And be there for a while

Then with the meaning of today
   I shall come back where I shall stay
and once again say "yes" to life!

And so each day I breathe in life
   Become the air—become the Light
And learn once more—life doesn't end
      Just changes

We travel forth becoming One
   With the earth and with the sun
We travel dancing with the air
   Shedding bodies and despair

For life and Love will never end
We just travel where we've never been
To learn to love again.

TO ALL MY KIDS

To all my kids on Mother's Day
   I wish to write a poem
And tell you of the Love I feel
   And pride I call my own

I'm sure it wasn't easy
   Growing up as one of six
But you have skills & memories
   That others often missed

You learned to tie each other's shoes
   Change diapers and clean rooms
While friends went down to the mall
   Bought toys and big balloons

You have memories of special winters
   When we had to sleep on floors
When shoveling coal & sleeping bags
   Became your daily chores

But you also do have memories
   Of simple times of fun
Of going on vacation
   Where you could swim & run

Now I look back on all those years
   And see a different light
I see bright and smiling faces
   Who giggle in the night

I see children sitting in church pews
   Beautifully in awe
Listening to stories
   Of things they never saw

I see Christmases around our tree
   And stockings by the fire
I hear melodies of lullabies
   Like angels in a choir

But most of all I see your Love
   So tender and so strong
A wondrous sense of family
   A place where you belong

I see children who are all grown up
   Giving Love in all they do
And I want to tell each special one
   How proud I am of you

So thank you for the gift of life
   That you have given me
For teaching me how to Love
   Which sets my Spirit free.

LOVE ANYWAY

In my life there was a time
  When all my thoughts were in my mind
I dreamt of all the good and bad
  And felt the fears of being sad

But now the freedom of my soul
  Has lifted me to being whole
Connected to the Force within
  Erasing all the signs of sin

Of simply being so in Love
  That's deep within and all above
Centered thoughts in my mind
  Projecting Love – another kind

And with her smile I live my life
  Supremely happy – with delight
      Loving anyway!

So go within and rest awhile
  Emerge in Love with a smile
Then you will laugh with all you do
  And know that You and I aren't two
      But One.

WINTER

Cool of winter coming forth
  Moving quickly with its force
Frosty nights painting scenes
  Upon the grass, upon the greens

Calling us to go inside
  Shorter days drifting by
Calling us to go within
  Crisp of winter now begins

Fires warming all our cares
  Resting in our favorite chair
Teaching us to take the time
  From our routine daily grind
      To Love

And in the calmness of this time
  I'll hear my heart and feel its rhyme
I'll go inside and hear my soul
  And see the stories being told

And make the changes in my mind
  I'll feel my heart and I will find
      Its Love.

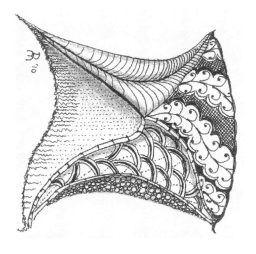

FOREVER

How do we begin to cope
  With loss of life with loss of hope?
How do we begin to bend
  From loosing such a mom & friend?

Our faith does teach that Love lives on
  And earth is just a path we're on
And then we pass into a place
  Of greater Love - of endless grace

And now for her peace has come
  Her Love lives on in everyone
So today when friends go home
  And we are left all alone

Just close your eyes and call her name
  She'll be right there - her Love's the same
And when you see her in your mind
  You'll be renewed with Love so kind

Her body's gone, but Love lives on
  Here on this earth and far beyond.

FOREVER

SILENCE

I will learn to love his Spirit
   As I've learned to love the change
I will calm my soul with his peace
   When only Love remains

But for now I'll try to comfort
   And ask what I can do
And someday I'll learn silence
   As I sit so close to you

For changes are occurring
   As parts now slip away
Like a slow motion picture
   As we watch another day

I will find so many ways of Love
   I never knew exist
I will simply learn "to be"
   And look forward to your bliss

Could you share what's going on
   Inside your silent mind
Could you give me the gift of words
   And calm these restless times?

Or could I learn to love you
   Just as you are today
And sit with you in silence
   In a new and joyous way.

THE NEXT PLACE

The next place that I go to
  Will be a place of Love
With warmth and sun and flowers
  Sent from up above

I'll take the Love within my heart
  And bring it right along
And recreate a life anew
  And sing a brand new song

I'll softly let my quiet voice
  Grow into a roar
And I'll surprise my very self
  As I begin to soar!

I'll take along the memories
  Leaving sadness far behind
I'll rediscover joy again
  In this brand new gift of time

I'll find a smile within my heart
  And Love within my soul
I know that I'll bring happiness
  For now I'm truly whole

I'll discover new adventures
  I can even make mistakes
In this brand new life I live
  In this brand new place

I'll wake up every morning
　　And kiss the rising sun
I'll smell the air and feel the wind
　　As I'm learning to have fun

It doesn't mean that I'll forget
　　My life before this date
I'll take it along with me
　　And make this new time great!

I don't know when I'll go there
　　I don't have the time or date
But I do know that this life begins
　　Each new day we awake!

SACRED SPIRIT

Sacred Spirit
  Giving birth
Within my soul
  To all the Earth

Unblocking all
  Our darkest parts
Filling Love
  For brand new starts

Simply giving
  Back to me
What always was
  For me to see

And as we watch
  The Earth just spin
We take a breath
  And go within

To see Your endless
  Burning Light
Which warms us whole
  Both day and night

Then we can see
  The moon and sun
And with our breath
  we are just One

Sacred Spirit

HAPPY MOTHER'S DAY

To everyone who's given Love
    Without ever asking why
To anyone who gives freely
    Both here – and those who've died

I express my gratitude
    To all who've given more
I am so very grateful
    For those who don't keep score

For some of us had a need
    That could not be fulfilled
And we remember grandmothers
    And aunts who filled the bill

All the teachers and the healers
    That came into our lives
Who taught the Love & filled the dreams
    Without ever asking why

So thanks to all the people
    Who've added to our Love
All the angels that He sent us
    To earth from up above

Some day we will remember
    Why we really came
So thank you all for being
    A part of that great plan

For really it's the nurturing
   And the Love you bring to earth
It's really not all about
   If you've given birth

Whether it's a dream or not
   In my heart I pray
For all of us – right here – right now

   HAPPY MOTHER'S DAY!

CHANGE

Sunlight resting
　On the branch
Untamed like
　An avalanche

But bringing warmth
　To things unseen
Showing seasons
　In between

Changes coming
　To our world
Some to find
　Within a pearl

Some are chosen
　Some are not
Some are longed for
　Some are sought

Within the darkness
　Of our minds
Some we choose
　To leave behind

But change will come
　And change will go
Teaching us
　That we can grow

　　With Love.

GRANDMOTHER'S PSALM

I saw them lifted into birth
   From her warmth
   Out on to earth

I saw them take their Ist new breath
   Then whisked away
   To be checked

I saw them struggle as they breathed
   Each new morning
   Into eve

I saw her watch with eyes of Love
   With only trust
   In up above

I saw the milk flow from her breasts
   Gently dripping
   On their chests

As they learned to suck and burp
   I watched their eyes
   and little quirks

And now I gaze at these two boys
   in cribs with quilts
   with stars and toys

And now I praise the moon and stars
   That decorate
   Their walls afar

And now I watch them as they grow
  And touch each little
  Hand and toe
    in wonderment

    These miracles of Life!

LOST GIFTS

Little one, little child
   Come and hold my hand a while
As we dream of scenes afar
   When you floated up on stars

Watch this precious girl and see
   How she learned to set her free
Free from feeling, free from pain
   Never to be hurt again

And while you floated up above
   I showered you with all my Love
I held your hand so you could dance
   Together we began to prance
        through fields of flowers

And in your silent days inside
   You seemed you loose your spark
   your drive
        -Not really

For a while your true heart slept
   Your gifts inside just took a rest
And now it's time to open wide
   Your special door & peek inside

Look inside and see your gifts
   So wondrous - they just lift
        Your soul
Always there - just waiting for
   The time that you would open doors

So step inside and look around
   Find a place and sit right down
I still am here to hold your hand
   To help you see and understand

So choose just one and pick it up
   And see excitement and great Love
This is YOU - my wondrous child
   Look around and gaze a while

     at LOVE.

MOTHER STUFF

All the years I dreamed she'd leave
    And freedom would be mine
But today a void which fills my heart
    Is like no other kind

For years ago I thought her words
    Came with a price to pay
I never thought her words to me
    Were any other way

Could she have really meant them
    With the wisdom of her years?
Could today her words of Love
    Wipe away my fears?

If she were here right now
    She'd say what's on her mind
But she would also love me
    With words both harsh & kind

Somehow back then I didn't hear
    The balance of those things
I dwelled on all the differences
    That life just sometimes brings

Today if she were to say
    "I love you - be a dear"
I'd hold on to the words of Love
    and let go of those I fear

For mothers are both honest
    And love you from their heart
It's too bad I didn't realize that
    From the very start

I spent so much time recording
    The differences we had
I spent so much time remembering
    The times she made me sad

But now with much more wisdom
    I look back on all those years
And realize that today she would
    Have wiped away my tears.

SPRING

Winter's coming to an end
　Spring is blooming once again
Buds on trees giving birth
　Blossoms bursting from the earth

All around us turning green
　The best of colors ever seen
Warmth of earth to plant our seeds
　And reap the beauty of our deeds

Longer days, shorter nights
　Enjoy the beauty, calm the fright
Little pansies with their heads
　Bowing to the showers shed

Standing tall with all their might
　Seeing birds in their flight
Little squirrels sorting nuts
　Hidden secrets in their huts

Birthing life has now begun
　Right out in the bright new sun
Slowly wonders find their way
　To bless each moment of our days

So touch the earth with our feet
　Ground our bodies to her beat
Becoming One with all of life
　Leaving winter and her nights

Take a moment, bathe in sun
　Spring is here — new life's begun!

GARDENS

I use to dream of gardens
   So very far away
With colors in the distance
   But I didn't know the way

I knew some day I'd go there
   but I couldn't find the path
And so I just began to walk
   Without a course or map

I knew if I kept going
   Around the mud and rocks
The beauty of the garden
   Would show within the blocks

Some days I walked this path alone
   Some days I cried for help
A hand to hold, some words of Love
   Would carry me through Hell

And then one day I saw it
   Coming near and near
My very precious garden
   With colors clear and dear

I stood there and just marveled
   At it's beauty deep and wide
I smelled it's fragrance, touched it's leaves
   Let go and gently cried

I thought the path was very long
   It's really very short
But there are clouds along the way
   That one must see and sort

The garden lies within your soul
   Its beauty is within
Just keep on walking down your path
   Let beauty now begin!

Walk down that path of clouds and mud
   For on the other side
You'll find your heart, and see your soul
   Your beauty and your pride!

WHEN I WAS YOUNG

When I was young & life begun
  I used to dance in leaves for fun
And then I grew and somehow knew
  I must behave and act like you

And so I watched all other's ways
  And skipped their steps down my maze
The road was long and damp and dark
  And I forgot my life - my spark

I moved with slow and careful steps
  So I would not have regrets
I was "good" and "oh so kind"
  I walked down life with my mind

But now I know that life just passed
  And I was free TO BE at last
I found the ME inside my mind
  And I am still sweet and kind

But now I dance to my new tune
  And visit many other rooms
I dance and skip and listen well
  To my heart where I now dwell

And deep inside I found my soul
  That gives me freedom - makes me whole
So come with me down this new land
  I'll be your friend - I'll hold your hand

          With Love.

GOD SAID

Do not ever be afraid
  For I am always here
To wash away your teardrops
  To calm your every fear

I am inside others
  And in the calm of night
I will whisper to you
  As the birds take flight

I am in the starlight
  And in your every breath
I will always hold you
  In life and in your death

For Love is always Sacred
  Holy is your name
I will always comfort you
  And take away your pain

So come with Me to this place
  Come and hold My hand
Together we will walk again
  Into a brand new plan.

AWAKEN

My heart is gently sleeping
   But feels His gentle arms
Holding all that's in me
   So near and yet so far

Holding all my stories
   Holding all my dreams
Awaken now, My child again
   Life is not what is seems

Awaken to your glory
   Awaken to new life
Remember all the colors
   Remember all that's right

Remember many pathways
   Remember how it was
Wipe away illusions
   Remember all My Love.

GRATEFUL

Grateful for the dreams we share
  And grateful for this time
Grateful for this picture
  And your Love of every kind

Grateful for the mornings
  Snuggling close in bed
Grateful for "I love yous"
  And the gentle words you've said

Grateful for your hand to hold
  As we sit and watch TV
Grateful for your warmth and Love
  As you sit so close to me

Grateful for this moment
  That I created, for I knew
That God is really in your eyes
  When I look at you.

LINGER IN THE MOMENT

Linger in the moment
  Of the memories and the bliss
Covered in the splendor
  Of kisses on our lips

Touches and caresses
  Of your fingers here & there
Saying yes to all the gifts
  God placed for us to share

Just two friends exploring
  The desires of our minds
And entering a sacred place
  Of passion so sublime

Riding waves of colored lights
  With dreams of wind & stars
Entering the Oneness
  Of Earth both near and far

And as we now rest and smile
  At this gentle day
When mere dictionary words
  Are not enough to say

Just linger in the moment
  Of this day and time
With heightened joys & feelings
  Of memories in our mind.

YOUR WEDDING DAY

Dearest one, my unborn child
  Sit with me and hear awhile
      The story of your Love

A story of a child so small
  Who listened to that tiny call

A helpless babe with half a hip
  Who changed my life—just a bit

Who taught me I could question God
  And gave me strength so I could trod
      Down the path of Love

Who overcame that one small plight
  And grew into a women bright
      And beautiful!

And now upon your wedding day
  We walk you down the aisle and say
      We love you—once again!

We give her to the man she loves
  God gives them grace from up above
      To walk their path of Love

So now begin this brand new life
  Take our child, make her your wife

And know that when you move away
  Our Love will follow every day

For love of souls and love of hearts
  Never fades and never parts

The story of the Love of souls
  Never ends— it just unfolds
      Again & Again.

PLAIN VANILLA DAYS

Nothing great, nothing new
  Just plain vanilla days
No flavors added to my life
  To color all my ways

No chocolate chunk or cherries
  Added to my soul right now
Just old familiar flavors
  Just promises and vows

Causing me to go within
  And seek a deeper soul
To find my Spirit, touch my God
  Who tells me I am whole

Then He can add the flavors
  Reminding me of ways
And walk with me in silence
  Through plain vanilla days.

BEGIN

The heaviness, the burdens
  That one time I embraced
Softly sometimes surface
  Bringing sadness to my face

And gently I'm reminded
  Of another time
When I floated up to pictures
  To protect my soul and mind

Years ago I began
  To truly let them go
Years of simply processing
  And walked into the flow

But tonight again the shape grew big
  I felt it hard and wide
It began to smother me
  And I had no place to hide

I painted it with color
  And felt the surface rough
Tonight I knew I'd made a choice
  Not to be so tough

I poked it with a needle
  And slowly it lost shape
It fell right down before me
  Like one big flat pancake!

It no longer was so heavy
   There was no air inside
Its life was truly gone from it
   I no longer had to hide

I picked it up so easily
   And held it in my hands
It crumpled right before me
   It fell amongst the sand

Then the wind came blowing
   And washed it out to sea
And Spirit walked up from the shore
   Embracing all of me.

CALLED BY SPIRIT

Called by Spirit
  To move again
Sometimes saying
  Good-bye to friends

Called by Spirit
  To the unknown
Trusting that
  You will be shown
    The way

Surrounded always
  By the Light
Breathing in
  All that's right

Feeling Spirit
  In our hearts
And welcoming
  Brand new starts

And so the circle
  Of this life
Brings us to
  A place that's right

For Love can never
  Be contained
And Love can never
  Remain the same

I wish you
  Love, Joy and Peace
As we let go
  And release you

    To new life

For You
  Are called by Spirit

CAN I

Within the clouds
  Of this day
I look to You
  As I pray

For signs & answers
  Deep within
Allowing me
  To now begin
    To change

Can I let go
  Of all my fears
That I've held
  For all these years?

Can I believe
  With all my heart
That I deserve
  A brand new start?

As I gaze
  At moon and sun
Do I believe
  I can have fun?

Can I accept
  A Love so kind
That sings each night
  Inside my mind?

Can I say "yes"
　　Within my soul
Can I believe
　　That I am whole?

As Bower Birds
　　Make their nests
For lovers
　　To come to rest

Fruits and nuts
　　Surround the hut
Flowers call
　　Their colors must

Attract a soul
　　To see what's real
Inside the nests
　　Of great appeal

Will she come
　　Will she look
Will she believe
　　In this new book?

Which tells the story
　　Of her heart
Does she believe
　　In brand new starts?

Can I trust
　　In Your great plan
And open up
　　To understand?

YES!

CHOICE

You can wallow in these feelings
　You can try them out for size
You can circle in self-pity
　You can watch TV & die

You can avoid the friends who call
　And never call them back
You can wander in these circles
　And always feel the lack

Or maybe as this time goes on
　You could begin some tears
Remembering all the Love you had
　And joy throughout the years

You could close your eyes & try real hard
　To see when you were young
You could remember just a bit
　Of how you had some fun

You could become a child again
　And give God one more try
You might discover joy again
　If you stop on asking why!

CHRISTMAS LOVE

Here it is - that time again
   Peace on Earth - Good Will Towards Men
Reminding us to Love and care
   For all mankind - everywhere

So as we shop and rush around
   Take a moment to calm down
And feel His Love inside of us
   See our gifts and stop the rush

Then we can sing and dance again
   And life becomes our long lost friend
When all of life becomes a dream
   Of lessons learned & those unseen

And Love will flow so easily
   To everyone we meet and see
And Christmas will begin to feel
   So alive - so very real

So quiet down - begin to start
   To feel your Peace & fill your heart

With Christmas Love

MOTHERS' VOICES

Mother's voices
  In our heads
Listening
  To what's been said

Singing songs of
  endless rhymes
Reminding us of
  other times

Can we hear our
  grown up voice
Telling us we
  have the choice

To keep these habits
  and these words
Even though they
  are absurd?

Or do we love
  ourselves enough
To shed these feelings
  and this stuff?

Release familiar
  times of past
Embracing freedom
  ours at last

To hug the child
  within my soul
And tell myself
  that I am whole
      & good
        & Lovable!

A VOICE

Today I found
   I had a voice
Hidden deep
   Within

It had a tiny
   Little sound
That wanted
   To begin

To get loud
   Just a little
And yell out
   On my own

To hold myself
   Straight and tall
And purge until
   I fall

And then with
   God's vibrations
I'll sing out
   On my own

And with this
   Voice of freedom
I'll never
   Be alone!

A WORLD BEYOND

Beyond this world
　Of things and flesh
There is a place
　Where we can rest

A place of joy
　A place of peace
Where worries of this
　World do cease

Where we remember
　Why we came
Where we no longer
　Feel our pain

Where the only name
　For God is Love
Where we awaken
　To above

And greet all those
　Who've gone before
Where we never
　Need much more

When we know
　Instead of feel
That everlasting life
　Is real

For I am in the
  Wind that blows
And in every seed
  You sow

I am part of all
  You see
I still live
  Just differently

For I am in the
  Setting sun
Reminding you
  We all are one

In this world
  Beyond all fear
I am always
  Very near

For I am just
  A thought away
And with your children
  As they play

And as you lay
  Your heads to rest
Remember – you
  Are always blessed

By this world beyond!

ABOVE THE CLOUDS

Looking down from up above
  And reflecting on your Love
I wonder if the clouds I see
  Are filled with possibilities

Did you see them on your path
  Did you dance in them at last
Did you curl up inside their mist
  Do they hold you in your bliss?

Is this endless sky of blue
  A mirror for both me & you
And can you hear me as I call
  Is God's Peace the same for all?

For now you know, while I still guess
  As my heart guides my quest
With clouds up high for all to see
  Connecting us eternally
      In Love.

MOTHER LOVE

If only I could
  Kiss your knee
And make it better
  So you could see

All the beauty
  Deep within
The Goddess
  Who will now begin

To rise up tall
  With answers sure
To linger in
  The very words

Written from
  All the minds
Collectively
  So you may find

Many choices
  Many songs
And instantly
  Where you belong

If only I could
  Hold your heart
And blanket all
  The injured parts

And carry all
  Your pain a while
Until you once again
  Could smile

If only I could
  Kiss your knee
And make you small
  Inside of me

And rock you
  Gently oh so safe
Until you found
  Your perfect place

But all I have
  Are love and ears
To lovingly caress
  And hear

To let you walk
  Into the woods
Forgetting all
  Advice and "shoulds"

To open doors
  Inside YOUR heart
To find out just
  How very smart
    You are

And so I blow
   A kiss to you
I cannot tell you
   What to do

I give you just
   A mother's Love
& from all woman
   Up above

Enormous Love
   So you may learn
Which way to go
   Which way to turn

JUST UNENDING LOVE!

I AM HERE

With all the years of wisdom
  That tell me I am here
With all the many lifetimes
  That were so sweet and dear

I'm called today to wonder
  With thoughts inside my mind
To listen to the Universe
  So I will clearly find

The messages I've hidden
  Deep within my heart
I will take the time today
  To let go and to start

Quieting my breathing
  Quieting my mind
Finding my own gentleness
  That I left behind

I will let go of all past thoughts
  And the future is not near
I will breathe into the present
  And find that I am here

And in this Holy Instant
  I'll feel the gentle sun
Clothe my mind and body
  As we become just One

Then every leaf and every tree
  Will speak their energy
And I will gladly open up
  To feel inside of me

Then filled with new forgiveness
  There will be no more fear
And once again I will believe
  That I am truly here

To learn the many lessons
  That I came on earth to see
And that I really have a choice
  To see things differently

For I am not the victim
  Of this world I see
And all the Love I need or want
  Is right inside of me!

IN AN INSTANT

"In your innocence
  My freedom lies"
Releasing me
  From all the ties

That held me bound
  That kept me closed
Amidst the stories
  And the prose

But now I see
  God's Love & Light
Rising forth
  Making bright

All the pictures
  In my mind
All the words
  Both harsh & kind

I put them in
  A red balloon
For in a while
  Very soon

I will let them go. . . .

The choice is mine
  When it should be
The choice is mine
  To set ME free

IN AN INSTANT

JOY

There is quiet joy in all we do
    As I sing and dance with you
We need not be loud in song
    Or dance about fast & strong

Joy can be within your heart
    When you choose a brand new start
It can be seen upon the bed
    Where little babies rest their heads

The joy of nature beckons me
    To see all that I can be
All flowers bow their heads & sway
    To the sunshine every day

Joy is stopping just a while
    To recognize a lover's smile
So look around at every thing
    See all the Joy that I can bring

        And Smile

LITTLE GIRLS

A little girl
  Alone in bed
Frightened by
  What had been said

Until an angel
  Did appear
Erasing all
  Her doubts & fears

The Light continues
  By her side
Knowing that
  This Love abides
    Within

For Lights & Love
  & rainbows
Aren't just
  For little girls

They grow into
  Acceptance
More precious
  Than all pearls

We hold this Love
  Within us
And give it
  Every day

To everyone
  God sends us
On our paths
  Along the way!

ONE YEAR AGO

One year ago
  We said our vows
And looking back
  From then to now

I reflect
  On so much more
The many paths
  We have explored

The times we've loved
  The times we've healed
The stories told
  Our thoughts revealed

The joyous growth
  Of knowing more
New moments given
  To explore
    New love

And now each day
  We're more aware
Of our choices
  And our prayers

For our Love is not
  Just you and me
But for all the world
  To see

And our choices
  We now know
Can help the world
  Begin to grow
    In Peace

And so again
  I do say "yes"
And promise you
  To give my best
    Of Love

SEE IT DIFFERENTLY

The words "to see it differently"
   Given in a dream
To explain a life of healing
   And what our stories mean

Then we can reach to others
   For in truth we are the same
We are in fact our brother
   With just a different name

The last of human freedom
   Is to choose our attitude
It is our Spirit's journey
   That we can choose our moods

As two raindrops joined together
   On the window of the glass
Are full but yet a moment
   And bring along the past

Then changed by wind they separate
   Much bigger than before
Sometimes it's really hard for us
   To see that we are more!

THE PEACE OF GOD

Nothing real can be threatened
   Nothing unreal exists"
All there is — is Love & Peace
   Do you believe in this?

A simple book of miracles
   Dictated to one mind
Teaching to remove all blocks
   Which we are led to find

Through how we treat our brother
   And how we see ourselves
Looking at our fears within
   And stories we have held.

And as the Light surrounds us
   A change just might occur
We might see things differently
   Forgiveness just might stir

It teaches us new lessons
   On how we treat our friends
It releases both the new & old
   And tells us "choose again"

For if I choose forgiveness
   I am choosing Love
And the quietness of my soul
   Awakens from above

And for an instant I remember
  Why I truly came
Each time I choose forgiveness
  I am never quite the same

I welcome each new morning
  And the lessons of the day
As I learn to think new thoughts
  I re-learn how to pray

Inside my heart there is a Voice
  That now I clearly see
Within my mind there is a song
  That always carries me

It lifts me up beyond the clouds
  And holds me in the Light
Erasing all the darkness
  Which colored many nights

For if there is just Love & Light
  Can fear be here & real
Or is it my illusion
  That I sometimes feel?

And if all of this is just a dream
  In a picture that I drew
Can I let go of everything
  That separates me from You?

For without this separation
  There is no guilt or sin
Without the past or future
  It's only NOW I'm in

For in a Holy Instant
   I can change my mind
Which leads me to a gentle path
   Where I will always find

THE PEACE OF GOD.

WHY WAS I BORN?

Why was I born
  why did I come
Why did I fly
  into earth & the sun?

Why did I float
  past the sky & her stars
How did we come
  to be where we are?

Questions come forth
  about time & its choice
Quieted by
  a familiar kind Voice

And breathing within
  we go to a place
Deep in our hearts
  of no time & no space

Accepting the Love
  remembering before
Filled with abundance
  and opening doors

So grateful for Life
  and the beauty of Earth
Embracing I AM
  and remembering my Birth!

HIGH UPON A HILL

High up in the country
   High upon a hill
Stands a farm all in white
   Where time is standing still

Enter here in silence
   For I'll give you words
To soothe your soul & calm your heart
   Like those you've never heard

I'll caress your body
   With lotions of delight
I'll take away your burdens
   And make your load so light

I'll free your path of all concerns
   And calm your weary mind
I'll feed you with my Spirit
   And aromas of all kinds

I'll give anything you ask of Me
   And free you of all ills
If you will only choose to come
   High upon the hill

I'll bathe you in new waters
   I'll set your spirit free
I'll open your eyes with new light
   So you can clearly see

I'll wrap you in new comfort
   All seasons will stand still
I will even breathe for you
   High upon the hill.

IF I COULD DREAM

If I could dream a dream for you
   I'd paint the sky a lovely blue
With puffy clouds so free and white
   With gentle breezes in the night

I'd paint a beach with sand so warm
   To comfort you amidst the storm
I'd give you angels in the night
   To sleep with you and make things right

I'd help you laugh and wipe your tears
   I'd gladly hold all your fears
But all I have is Love to give
   To comfort you as you live
      One more day.

NOTHING IS THE SAME

If only I had never
  Opened up the Book
If only I had never
  Dared to take a look

And began to read the lessons
  Each and every day
And even went & joined a group
  And found a brand new way

I wouldn't be so frustrated
  When anger surfaced forth
My mind wouldn't quote to me
  Lessons from the Course

And I could still just wallow
  Blaming others for my fate
And I could gather witnesses
  Proving I should hate

They were wrong & I was right
  In my drama play
And I could just continue
  Doing things MY way

But "no" I was a lucky one
  Who in an angel store
Found this Book with promises
  That life was so much more

So now my life has changed a bit
    Since there's no sin or fear
Even when my ego's
    Ugly head does rear

I can no longer wallow
    In my stories & my blame
The Course has changed all of that
    Nothing is the same!

        Damn It

NOW

There is no future or the past
  We only have the NOW
Artists know this in their hearts
  Not asking why or how

They simply lift their brush to paint
  And then the beauty flows
And writers slowly open up
  With words they've never known

We only have this moment
  We only have what is
If we can simply listen
  We'll catch glimpses of this bliss

The rest is just a drama
  It's only just a play
We get to be the actors
  We only have today

So on this day, this moment
  I will quiet all my mind
And drift into an instant
  Suspended free of time

And in this place of quiet
  I'll let go of "little me"
Thoughts will simply disappear
  So I can truly BE.

FRIENDS

As these words roll to an end
   And I reflect on where I've been
I gently see within my heart
   And call to mind so many parts

I look ahead with so much hope
   To live life well - not just to cope
But most of all I thank my friends
   Who've walked with me & where I've been

For this great life is such a gift
   We get to choose; we get to lift
      ourselves to wonder

But one thing that will never end
   We get to walk this road with friends!
In all the books and all the poems
   We never walk this road alone

And so for you & all who see
   The many varied parts of me
I thank you all for this day
   And for your Love along the way!

NOTES:

9011782R0

Made in the USA
Charleston, SC
03 August 2011